INDEX

TOLEDO: A SHORT CUT

I

The shadows are creeping along the olive groves and the Tagus begins to sing its song. Only at dusk can the deep, rhythmic, immortal waters of the Tagus be heard.

Slowly, ever so slowly, I walk down one of the countless paths, so typical of Toledo, which begin at the doorways of the *cigarrales* (country homes), pass by the old hermitages and end up at the San Martín and Alcántara bridges. Like tiny brooks which flow humbly into the larger river, these are short cuts to the Tagus.

II

What do we see and what do we experience along the way? It slips along like an artery, among the *cigarrales*. Almost all of the *cigarrales*, country mansions, are the same, surrounded by olive trees. The tall Catalonian olive tree, the Andalusian olive tree, the Balearic olive tree, coarse and twisted like a flamenco dance. The Toledo olive tree is not like the others. It is delicate, full of harmony and sweetness. It is more like the olive trees of Florence or the Holy Land. The olive tree, to us, is Peace personified.

III

We stop at a little hermitage. The smell in the air is very different there. The rockrose, the flower of the fields; the odor of the farmers, who smell of corduroy, sweat, horses and bran. The foul odor of the cheap oil of the taverns and the tart smell of the wineskins in the patios of the inns. The rancid odor of the old stones of the castles, weighed down with centuries of history. The smell of straw. The smell of wine and the grape. The smell of the bull. The woman who smells like a woman.

The damp odor, perfumed with incense, from the depths of the cathedrals. And this smell of wax and thyme belonging to the small hermitages, protected by the rises of the *cigarrales*. The smell, the smell of Spain!

IV

The *cigarraleros* (those who live and work in the *cigarrales*) with their burros trudge up and down the paths. And silent women, loaded down with bread and cheese and bottles of wine so red that it appears to be black. And dark, happy children, who are always rushing about.

Everything gives the sensation of movement, of migration. But no. These people neither come nor go. They have been there forever and so they will remain. They are as deeply rooted into the earth as the olive trees. The road takes me past a noble mastiff, the noblest of all the dogs. He approaches me and sniffs and then looks up with his two-colored eyes. He wags his tail and wanders off contentedly. He has done his duty.

TOLEDO

HISTORY, COLOR AND ART

ERISA

Ediciones y Reproducciones Internacionales S.A.

© ERISA
Pol. Ind. II - La Fuensanta - Edif. Grefol
Móstoles (Madrid). Telf.: 645 74 66
Especial thanks to: Fredeswindo González Ortega
Texts: J. M.ª Fernández Gaytán. Pablo M. Valdés and Luis Alba
ISBN: 84-85844-22-X
Depósito Legal: M. 26.157-1985
Printed by GREFOL, S. A., Pol. II - La Fuensanta
Móstoles (Madrid)
Printed in Spain

We reach the San Martín bridge and we can admire once again its aged skeleton. The waters flow below the bridge on their way to the Atlantic. They are noisy, like a fraternal and emotional farewell to the venerable city, whose past glories still echo like the roar of the ocean in a conch shell.

The short cut is the path which shortens the route; we must follow. And the whole art of living is made up of just that: of shortening the roads we take...

VI

I have left my beloved little path behind and once more —I have done it so often in my already long life!— I have taken a long walk through the streets of Toledo. The Alcázar; the Cathedral; El Greco's house; the Tránsito Synagogue; Santa María la Blanca; San Juan de los Reyes; Zocodover, the calle de Santo Tomé, which is the street of "The Burial of Count Orgaz" —El Greco's masterpiece— and also the street of the delicious marzipans; so many palaces as that of Fuensalida, with its long history; so many churches and monuments; so many vestiges of the three great Toledo cultures: Arabic, Jewish and Christian...

I first became familiar with this eternal wonder, as a child, holding my father's hand, like any other Toledan. All of this is magnificently reflected in this book of which its publishers can be truly proud. The beauty of the photographs; the perfect synthesis of its comments; the skilled selection and preparation of this work, have given us a concrete and admirable impression of the «History, Color and Art of Toledo.»

Doctor Marañón, for whom Toledo was his great love, would have cherished it. Among his last words, before his death, were: "Toledo light of my life."

This is the image of Toledo that Editorial Erisa has given us: LIGHT.

GREGORIO MARAÑON MOYA
Ambassador of Spain

Bisagra gateway.

THE BISAGRA GATE

The Traveller has no less than nine choices for entering Toledo, nine gateways leading into the heart of the walled-in area. However, of all of the gates, the largest and most important is the Puerta Nueva de Bisagra (New Bisagra Gate).

A majestic facade constructed in 1550 by Covarrubias in order to receive King Carlos I, and later expanded by Felipe II, it consists of two solid keeps with embrasures for cannons in the lower section. The doorway itself is set between both keeps, above which is the enormous coat of arms of Carlos V, carved out of granite, and featuring the bicephalous eagle in the background.

On the side facing the city is the coat of arms of Toledo. Two towers crowned with beautiful spires are covered with glazed tiles showing the Imperial coat of arms.

Inside is a patio where we can see the image of St. Eugene, perched above the doorway; to one side is a statue of Carlos V.

The name of this gate is of Arabic origin and refers to the peasants who passed through here on their way home from a day's work in the rich fields of red earth (La Sagra). In Arabic, Bisagra is Bib-Sahla, which means Door to the countryside. However, there were also those who sought to bestow a Latin, Roman origin on the Gate by claiming that the city's Via Sacra began here.

The Bisagra gateway as seen from the Puerta del Sol.

The new Bisagra gateway.

Statue of Carlos V.

Church of
Santa Leocadia.

Bisagra gateway.
Interior facade.

The old
Bisagra gate.

The ramparts stand behind the statue of Alfonso VI.

THE RAMPARTS

There is another gate nearby which is older. Tradition has it that King Alfonso VI entered the city here to reconquer it from the Moors on May 25, 1805.

It is a very noble structure, dating back to the tenth century most likely, with an incipient mudejar style even though the horseshoe arch and the lower sections are clearly Arabic.

Set on an old Roman roadway, the old Bisagra gate is found in the Arabic walled-in area. The Torres de la Reina (Towers of the Queen) belonged to this area, along with the remains of the city walls which begin at Alcántara and end at the Renaissance Puerta del Cambrón gate. Inside this gate is the image of Santa Leocadia which is attributed to Berruguete.

The visitor who enters Toledo through the Puerta de Bisagra, as we have suggested, and continues along the Arrabal de Santiago, will almost necessarily reach the Puerta del Sol, with its perfect mudejar style, its seductive brick structure. From here, we can contemplate the gentle flow of the Tagus River which is called the "feet" of Toledo.

Two unusual items must be seen in the Puerta del Sol square. One is the coat of arms of the Cathedral of Toledo, which is framed in a triangle, located in the smallest of the interior arches; in the largest arch, we see an attractive sculpture which was probably taken from a Christian sarcophagus. Located off to the right and farther up, we have the Valmardón Gate, which is also called the Puerta del Cristo de la Luz, because the mosque of the same name is found very close-by. This gate is also very old and its construction reflects the military influence on the medieval city.

he gateway. The rear facade.

The ramparts and the Provincial Government building in the background.

Typical houses near the Church of Santiago del Arrabal.

The site of La Cava's bath.

Statue of the Emperor Carlos V.

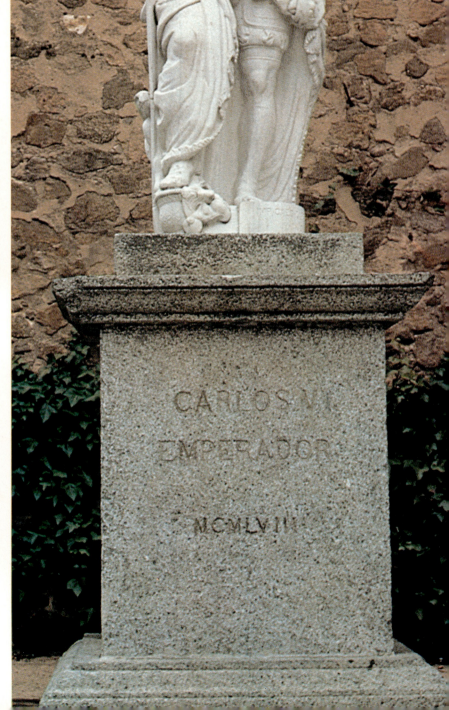

The Alcántara bridge.

THE BRIDGES

Two very old bridges span the Tagus on both sides of the city. The Alcántara bridge to the East and the San Martín bridge to the West. The Alcántara, the oldest of Toledo's bridges, was constructed by the Arabs in the year 866

or thereabouts. Nevertheless, we do not see it today in its original form, for it had to be reconstructed in 1257 and that is when it adopted its present form of two arches and two towers.

In the opposite direction is the San Martín bridge, of a more recent construction (XIII-XV cents.), and its five arches give it a magnificent, solid and symmetrical appearance.

The bridge is finished off at either end by two keeps; one which faces Toledo and bears, in bas-relief, the coat of arms of the city; and the other, which leads us to the *cigarrales* on the outskirts of the city and where we see the image of Archbishop San Julián.

The Alcántara bridge is poetry even in its name, which in Arabic means "the bridge", "the arch". Its location appears to be unique and indispensable for a few meters away stood the old Roman bridge which ancient battles and the inexorable passage of time have destroyed.

The ninth century Arab bridge had also been demolished during the flooding of the Tagus River and King Alfonso X is to be thanked once again for its reconstruction. It has not remained untouched over the subsequent years either for it was necessary to repair the structure in the 15th and 18th centuries and twice in the present one.

There, beside the San Servando Castle, the hieratic stone watchman of history and a contemporary of the bridge, give or take a few years, the noble Alcántara represents an obliged visit if we wish to unearth the real and profound truth behind the Imperial city. In any case, we will guard, with prudential care, some of the thousand and one indecipherable mysteries concealed behind the demure, virginal design.

At the opposite end of town, at a 180º angle, stands the San Martín bridge, whose past history has also been conflictive, ranging from its construction in the 13th century to its reconstruc-

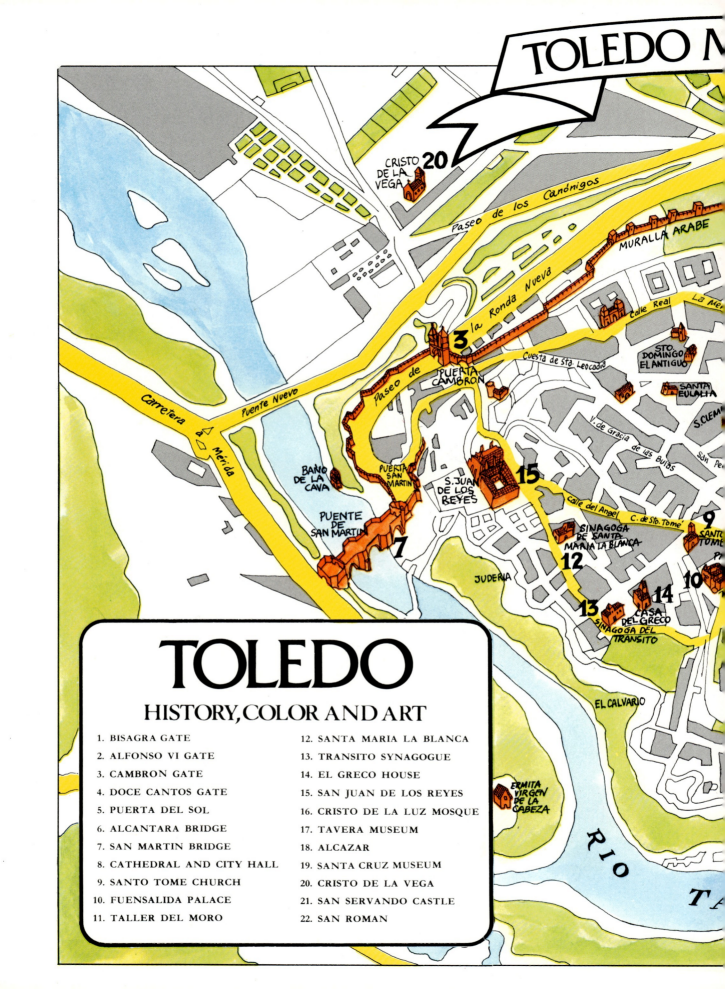

TOLEDO

HISTORY, COLOR AND ART

NUMENTAL

17 MUSEO DE TAVERA

1 → A MADRID

O VI

PUERTA DE BISAGRA

SANTIAGO DEL ARRABAL

PUERTA NUEVA

Real del Arrabal

PTA. DE ALARCONES

5 PUERTA DEL SOL

STO. DOMINGO EL REAL

CRISTO DE LA LUZ

16

19

6 PUENTE DE ALCANTARA

21 CASTILLO DE SAN SERVANDO

de la Rosa

CENTRO UNIVERSITARIO

SAN NICOLAS

S. VICENTE

PLAZA DE ZOCODOVER

MUSEO DE STA. CRUZ

C. de Cervantes

ILDEFONSO

Calle de la Plata

Alfonso X

Paseo

onso XII

Calle del Comercio

18

DOCE CANTOS

4

Calle de la Trinidad

ALCAZAR

ADOR

SAN MIGUEL

8 CATEDRAL

PLAZA DEL AYUNTAMIENTO

Calle S. Marcos

SANTA URSULA

Calle del Barco

SAN JUSTO

AN RTOLOME

Calle del Pozo Amargo

SANTA ISABEL

CANDELARIA

SAN LUCAS

Circunvalación

SAN ANDRES

SAN SEBASTIAN

DE SAN SEBASTIAN

STA. CATALINA

Cinturón de

Cinturón de Circunvalación

San Martín bridge.

tion two centuries later, carried out by the Archbishop Tenorio. Its five arches are of matchless, solid beauty, representative of the city which it unites and protects. Pedro I and Enrique de Trastamara, his brother, were responsible for carrying out the necessary work which affected the maximum tensor of the bridge in a very special manner.

The bridge has two fortified towers of formidable, belicose design, which were intended to ward off enemy invasions and at the same time, stand tall as a symbol of the courage and gallantry of the city. Today it conserves the granite image of the Virgen del Sagrario and the solitary figure of the Archbishop San Julián. Together they represent the peace and serenity of Toledo, a city to which one must come with an open heart and a receptive spirit, in order to fully appreciate its history which is alive in every corner,

every street and every monument of Toledo.

First, it is absolutely necessary for the visitor to view Toledo from the other side of the Tagus, from any of the look-out points which stand out along the Altos del Valle today. Then, we must descend to the bridge which will take us to the favorite gate of the Roman, Visigothic, Arabic, Castilian ramparts, which, like all Toledo, are also Jewish, and we can make our entrance thusly into the city.

It is one of the most unique views in the world with its golden patina, of old and beloved gold, purified over the centuries by the passage of so many races, religions and cultures. It is a visit which we will cherish eternally as an unperishable souvenir of the soul, which becomes for a brief instant a roll of film which we hope will last forever.

The visitor is now in Toledo.

San Martin bridge.

San Martin bridge.

San Martin bridge.

Alcántara bridge.

15

San Martín bridge.

Alcántara bridge.

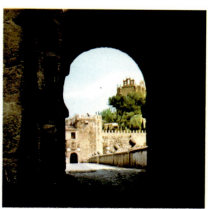

San Martín bridge.

*San Servando Castle
the Alcántara bridge.*

A typical street (San Marcos).

Toledo is, without a doubt, a city which has been the cradle of cultures and in its urban morphology, it gives us over and over again, a complete history lesson which it has experienced throughout its evolution: the Roman epoch, the Visigothic, the Arabic, the Mozarabic, the Mudéjar and the Christian. There is no other city in the world which can offer the visitor such incomparable wealth. It is the most suggestive summary that anyone can obtain of Spain and its history.

Cossío said that "Toledo is the city which is a spectacle of civilizations, piled one on top of another and whose remains co-exist to form countless churches and convents, Gothic, Mudéjar and Plateresque dwellings, steep narrow streets of Moorish flavor; an almost living and intact painting of a town where each stone is a voice which speaks to the spirit."

Four hundred years of history remain untouched by the passage of time and they make us think, as we wander along the steep, narrow "tiny streets" —as the great writer Azorín defined them that we are right in the middle of the sixteenth century. Everything has remained unchanged!

And yet, we open our eyes and there is the civilization of our days, the business, the noise, the traffic and hordes of tourists who come to Toledo. We are abruptly brought back to the reality of the world of today, the world in which we live.

But the visitor walks on. He follows the incredible urban routes which take him along alleys in which he need barely reach out to touch the buildings on either side; steep paths which are difficult to climb; peaceful hidden corners where our dreams become lost in time; mysterious paths which twist and wind around the hill like Cretan laberinths; small streets which make our hearts beat widely from exhaustion, excitement and a confusing reverential fear of intruding upon a past which we would

THE CITY

Toledo, that marvelous island traced out by the Tagus river in the form of an eagle, with wings outstretched to the severe fields of Castile, as a kind of isthmus. A privileged city with a superb location 527 meters above sea level on a rock, divided in some hills, which is surrounded by the magnificent meander of the Tagus on all except the north side, where the river carved out a deep rocky gorge.

Zocodover square.

get the strange feeling that the experience is mutual, that those tiny, winding, timeless streets, seem to want to reach out and touch us, hug us and keep us company throughout our route.

And the entire framework of the Toledo streets leads us, repeatedly, to the very heart and core of the city, to its main square, the Zocodover, the Suk-al-Dawab or Market of the Beasts, to the Mozarabic Gocodoeb of eight centuries ago, to the square of the Arco de la Sangre (Arch of Blood), where a Christian chapel of the same name had stood at the end of the 16th century. There are many who believe, and they are perhaps right, that the only way to get to know a city is by walking a long its streets. The major artistic attractions, they add, rarely relate to the soul of the people. And this is especially true in Toledo, aside from the incomparable treasures which have led it to be recognized as the city of art "par excellence" in the whole world.

As we move from street to street, house to house, we travel through centuries and centuries as if we were transported by a special time machine, to the Court of Tagus, descendent of King Tubal, who gave his name to the river; or to the Jewish Toledoth, or the Hebrew Toledath, which means "Generations" or "Mothers of peoples"; to the Roman Consul Tolemón, Toletum, Tolaitola; until we arrive at Cervantes's "most precious jewel" in the crown of what was the most powerful nation in the world.

The visitor walks along and penetrates into the laberinth of Toledo streets and little by little, he begins to identify with what he is seeing. This is because Toledo never remains distant or foreign to the visitor; rather it penetrates our very soul, until we experience an incredible symbiosis, which will make us feel like an integral part of the city itself. And that sensation, which is certainly gratifying, will remain with us always. Let us continue our stroll.

not, under any circumstances, wish to offend.

The visitor walks and walks along the narrow streets which will help him get to know Toledo that much better, and at the same time, get to know himself in relation with the city. For as our walk progresses, we will

alle de las Airosas with the old Bisagra gate in the background.

Cathedral: Door of the Kings (Puerta de los Reyes).

THE CATHEDRAL

The Cathedral can be considered, perhaps, the most important monument in a city which is in and of itself, a monument. Work on the Cathedral was begun in the year 1227, when Fernando III the Saint placed the first stone for its construction. The building follows the cannons of French Gothic but in its design, one can really appreciate the Spanish spirit, reflected in the mighty, solid lines of its walls. It has five naves: the central apse is 45 meters high and it is here that the beautiful choir of resplendent Gothic style is found. The four lateral naves surround the main altar and open into a series of small chapels.

But before we go inside the Cathedral, the visitor should take a leisurely walk around the exterior of the structure in order to admire its doorways, among which we must single out for special contemplation, the Puerta de los Leones (Door of the Lions). It was contructed in the 15th century by Anequín Egas in flamboyant Gothic style and it takes its name from the lions carved in marble, which decorate it. A little farther on, is the famous Puerto Llana, which is of more recent construction (1800). It is from this doorway that the Monstrance of the Cathedral departs in a procession through the streets of the city, every Corpus Christi day.

Our walk around, the outside of the temple ends at the main facade, which opens into three doorways: That of the Torre (Tower), the Juicio (Judgment) and, in the center, that of the Perdón (Forgiveness), which is the most beautiful of all due to its pointed arches and its elaborate decoration in which the twelve Apostles appear in detailed relief along with the scene depicting the Virgin presenting San Ildefonso, Patron Saint of the city, with the Chasuble.

Once we are inside, we must forget time and our watch. We must pause to admire the stained glass windows, the frescoes of the cloister, the exaggerated Churrigueresque work in the Transparente, the diversity of styles found in the numerous chapels, the Chapter House, the beautiful choir and sacristy, converted into a museum.

And, finally, we cannot afford to miss the Treasury, the room containing the art and relics, in order to have a close look at the exquisite Monstrance, by Enrique Arfe, a splendid piece of gold and silver smithery, standing three meters high, with a weight of 200 kilos. The entire piece is made of silver and gold which is thought to be the first gold brought by Columbus from the Americas.

However, a complete guide for a visit to the Cathedral of Toledo, which is

The apse aisle.

considered by many to be the most important in Spain, would take more pages than we have available in the entire book. We are not going to visit it then with the detailed inspection of an expert but rather with the love and admiration which it inspires in any of the thousands of people who visit it each day.

We can begin at the Santa Catalina Doorway, which like the Plateresque Presentación Doorway, opens into the Cloister of the Cathedral. The image of St. Catherine presides over the central column of black marble which divides the Gothic arch of the doorway. The frescoes of the lower gallery offer us a series of scenes in the lives of the Saints and we fine here eleven Bayeus and one Maella (another one was lost).

We think that Petrus Petri, its first architect, initially designed a building 113 meters long and 57 meters wide, with 88 pillars, opened into five naves, receiving light from the 750 stained-glass windows.

The Cathedral embraces, integrates and combines a series of impressive chapels. If we enter the temple through the Mollete doorway, we will see a long series of chapels, among which we must make special mention of the Ochavo (embellished with such relics as two thorns of the Crown of Thorns of Christ or the ashes of Santa Leocadia and San Eugenio), Santa Lucía (called today "Sagrado Corazón", Sacred Heart, with paintings by Caravaggio and Maella, the Epiphany, the Mozarabic chapel, dating back to the 16th century, whose cult follows the Gothicor Isidorian missal and breviary rather than the Gregorian books, and finally the old chapel of the San Juan Tower which is today the Treasury Room. The "fat bell" or "Saint Eugene", in its position high above the square tower, deserves special attention. It measures nine and a half meters at its perimeter and weighs 17,500 kilograms.

Cisneros founded the Chapter House. Its construction was carried out between 1504 and 1512 with a Gothic doorway by Copín of Holland; a mudejar coffered ceiling with the classic eight-point star and frescoes by Juan de Borgoña, who is also responsible for the series of portraits in the upper section which range from St. Eugene to Cisneros himself, a collection of paintings which is brought up-to-date in the lower section by contemporary artists of each prelate. (Goya, Vicente López, Francisco Ricci, Luis Tristán or Francisco Comontes.)

Behind the magnificent Plateresque grille which was the work of Francisco de Villalpando for the Main Chapel, the heart of the temple with the Choir, we find ourselves opposite an incomparable altarpiece which covers the entire front section of the Chapel, and which

in Altar.

Cloister and Santa Catalina Doorway.

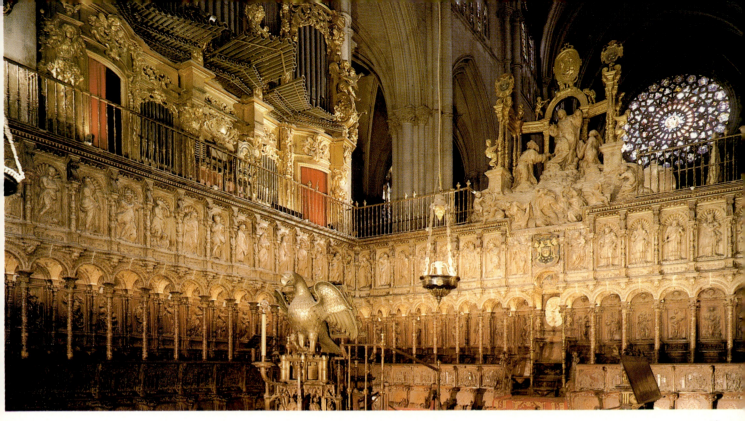

Choir. ⇉

is owed to the initiative of Cardinal Cisneros. It seems that 27 of the best artists of the period carried out this commission during a period of four years of uninterrupted work. Among the artists, we can name Copín of Holland, Petit-Jean, Cumiel, Egas and others, who jointly achieved one of the best samples of elaborate Gothic in all Europe, and for many, the best altarpiece on the continent.

The Choir is also found in the heart of the building. The retrochoir, which we can reach via the main doorway, is also of florid Gothic, with a central medallion by Berruguete, representing God surrounded by the Evangelists. It is said that the Choir grille, the work of Domingo Céspedes, led to the bankruptcy of the artist, who apparently made a mistake when he submitted his bid for the work. Professional pride prevented him from rectifying his estimate and he died in poverty after having spent his personal fortune in creating his great work of art.

Felipe de Borgoña and Alonso de Be-

rruguete shared the task of constructing 70 seats for the upper choir stall gallery in Renaissance style and Maese Rodrigo carved 50 seats of walnut for the lower section. He depicted such scenes as the Conquest of Granada, by the Catholic Monarchs and figures of animals, both real and imaginary.

Two hundred thousand ducats were spent on the "Transparente", whose construction was completed in 1732, after twelve long years of work. Archbishop Diego de Astorga y Céspedes can be credited with supporting this project and for this reason, he was buried in the chapel. Painter, sculptor and architect, Narciso Tomé, with the help of his children, carried out this monumental task which is the height of Spanish Churrigueresque style, a symphony of marble, bronze and alabaster. The Transparente was able to break the monotony of the temple without endangering the stability of its parts and it allows for direct light to enter and accentuate the impressive profiles of the structure.

"The kiss of Judas", by Goya.

THE SACRISTY

Carducio and Caxés, with their paintings in the anteroom of the Sacristy, lead the way into the main salon, which we must visit for it is an exceptional picture gallery above which unfolds the huge fresco painted by Lucas Jordán. We see "The arrest" or "The kiss of Judas", by Goya; the portrait of Cardinal Borja, by Velazquez; the "Holy Family", "Santa Inés and the portrait of Pope Inocencio IX, by Van Dyck; "San Diego de Alcalá", by Ribera; a "Crucifixión" by Titian; the cardboard drawings for the Teniers tapestry; and a great selection of works by El Greco: "San Francisco", "The Tears of St. Peter", thirteen paintings of his first series of the Apostles, including a painting of Jesus, and the self portrait of the painter in the very first of the series, as St. Luke, and the "Spoliation", which presides the Sacristy.

Painted in 1577, the red tunic of the Savior strikes us as an explosion of love which flows gently, deeply and fraternally, from the cluster of heads which make up the background of the painting, instead of the more commonly used clouds, sky or countryside. They reflect in the eyes of Jesus, the infinite love of a centuries-old doctrine and lesson.

Portrait of Cardinal Borja, by Velázquez.

Fragments of the St. Louis Bible.

"Bible of Saint Louis", illustrated on this page, which receives its name because of the fact that it was a gift from the Sainted King of France. It has miniature paintings carried out on more than five thousand gold leaves. We should not overlook the wooden cross, painted by Beato Fra Angelico, the St. John the Baptist, carved by Martínez Montañés, the chalice donated by Marshall Petain, and an endless list of other treasures.

And above all, of course, is the Monstrance which we will see on the next page, the work of gold and silver-smith Enrique de Arfe. He took more than seven years to complete the job which Cardinal Cisneros had commended to him. It contains approximately 5,600 parts, held tightly in place, according to Sixto Ramón Parro, by 12,500 screws.

THE TREASURY, COLLECTION OF RELICS AND ART

Before we leave the Cathedral, we should visit the old chapel located at the base of the large tower. It later became the sacristy of the Chapel of the New Monarchs and, after a period of restoration intended to convert it into Cardinal Tavera's mausoleum (who would later choose the Hospital which would bear his name), it became the Treasury Room. We enter through the Plateresque Doorway, the work of Alonso de Covarrubias.

Among the countless and priceless pieces that are kept here, we should first point out the three volumes of the

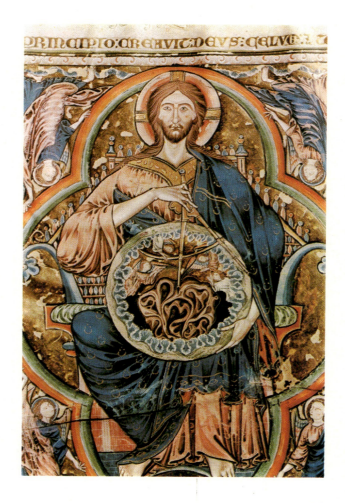

Fragment of Greco's masterpiece.

THE CHURCH OF SANTO TOME

This temple was raised upon the ruins of an old Arab mosque. Gonzalo Ruiz de Toledo, Señor de Orgaz, who died in 1323, was responsible for its construction and his death is immortalized in El Greco's masterpiece, "The Burial of Count Orgaz". The temple also has a beautiful mudejar tower.

And once again, we must return to the sphere of the legends. It is said that when the Count died in 1323 and he was about to be buried Saint August and Saint Stephan, for whom the Count had felt special predilection, appeared.

It was the Saints who placed the mortal remains of the Count in his tomb, while a deep voice was heard to proclaim: "This is the reward for he who serves God and his Saints."

Two centuries later, parish priest Andrés Núñez de Madrid commissioned El Greco to paint a scene which would perpetuate this legend and it took the painter two years to complete the task.

In the painting, the communion between life on earth and the Glory is established. Both parts, the lower and upper sections respectively, are perfectly differentiated. Above, the celestial court; below, the two Saints holding the body of the Count before a group of people whose faces have been associated with real historical personnages of the period.

Thus, we have another unsolved mystery in Toledo because we find a series of coincidences in these names.

First, in the part of the Glory, we see the Saviour, Mary, St. John the Baptist, and St. Peter. To the right, among the clouds, we can make out Hell. Just about in the geometric center of the painting, an Angel is holding a diffused form which symbolizes Don Gonzalo's soul.

On the earthly plane, people have tried to see Felipe II in the painting. Perhaps. But the only real assurance that we have seems to lean, apart from the afore-mentioned Saints who appear from left to right, towards the painter himself, depicted above St. Stephen's head. It is the only figure in the painting which looks straight ahead, at least in this area. His son, Jorge Manuel, who years later would become an important architect of the city, appears as the page in the foreground to the left, and the priest who is reading the prayer book at the far right, would be the priest himself who had commissioned the work.

The painting is a song to Salvation and is without a doubt, one of the milestones of universal art.

Detail of the Fuensalida Palace.

In the other palace, the Taller del Moro, we should single out the Mudejar beauty of its coffered ceilings and artistic plaster work, in addition to the ceramic and Moslem art objects which are on display in the rooms, which serve as a museum today.

The palace has a long and important history which begins with Pedro López de Ayala, the Count who built the Palace which now bears his title. It is commonly believed that here between the noble and austere walls, Isabel of Portugal died in 1539. More recently, the building took on a military role and nowadays it is the headquarters for the Autonomous Government.

Even though the second palace had been used as a storehouse and even as a place for the preparation of the different materials to be used in the building of the Cathedral, its valuble decoration leads us to believe that in another period, it was an integral part of a greater and more important palace. It might even have belonged to the Count and Countess of Fuensalida.

It has a very pure Grenadine Mudejar style. Its plaster decoration is exquisite and its rooms contain the finest artisan work: ceramic panels, small studded chests, Cordovan travel chests, red earthen-ware vats with handles, green glazed fountains, friezes, moldings, wells, beams, mortars and a long list of other attractions.

Geographically connected and perhaps joined by history a hundred times over, the Palace of Fuensalida and the Taller del Moro are exemplary witnesses to some of the most significant pages of Toledo's history, a city which has known how to care for and lovingly conserve its Past, in order to be able to offer us today a clean and diaphanous record of what Man has achieved in his advancement towards Eternity.

FUENSALIDA PALACE AND THE TALLER DEL MORO

Very close to the Church of Santo Tomé are two old palaces. One is Christian, the Palace of the Fuensalida, and the other is Moorish. Both structures are almost joined to one another.

The Palacio de Fuensalida was constructed in 1440 and represents the classic lay-out of the Renaissance urban palace, but, in truth, in it, all of the different styles of the city are blended: it has Gothic touches, Plateresque decorations and, above all, Mudéjar elements.

"The Burial of the Count of Orgaz", by El Greco.

Patio of the Fuensalida Palace.

Taller del Moro.

Baptismal font.

The garden of El Greco's house.

THE HOUSE AND MUSEUM OF EL GRECO

El Greco lived and worked in Toledo and as he assimilated the environment, he was then able to reflect it so masterfully on canvas. The city, in gratitude, is dedicated to honoring the name of the brilliant Greek artist. Set in the old Jewish quarter, the Casa del Greco is maintained thanks to the efforts of the Marqués de Vega Inclán. The entrance in the hall leads directly to the inner patio. During the visit, we can admire not only many of the artist's works which decorate the walls, but we can get the feeling of the atmosphere which inspired his work.

Before it was purchased by El Greco, the original palace, constructed by Samuel Levi, had belonged to the Marqués de Villena. In the Museum, we can see the last of the series of Apostles, for which M. B. Cossio and Gregorio Marañón accept the tradition that El Greco used, as models, the patients from the nearby insane asylum of Nuncio.

There are, of course, several paintings of San Francisco, with whom El Greco was especially impressed and other interesting works. Deserving special mention is the "Plano de Toledo" (Map of Toledo) in which the Hospital de Afuera is carried in a cloud to the center of the city, because as Marañón explained, "it did not fit into the composition of the painting."

El Greco arrived in Toledo in 1577 and he is perhaps the foremost of all the mysteries of Toledo. A. M. Campoy considered him "the most enigmatic painter of all times". The House and Museum of El Greco allows us to penetrate into his memory and identify ourselves directly with his life and his painting.

"A view of Toledo", by El Greco.

"St. Peter", by El Greco.

"St. Paul", by El Greco.

40

Column capital in the Santa María la Blanca Synagogue.

SANTA MARIA LA BLANCA

THE JEWISH CULTURE. THE SYNAGOGUES

When we speak of Toledo, we must necessarily make mention of the Jewish community which lived there and left the city two precious gifts, its Synagogues.

The Synagogues naturally reflect part of the city's glorious past for many chapters of Toledo's history are clearly marked by the Hebraic influence.

Though well-known are the trials and vicissitudes, the ups and downs experienced by the Synagogues and the Jewish communities over the years and throughout the different epochs, these magnificent monuments still represent what Toledo has always stood for: *Toledancia*.

The visitor will certainly be surprised when he enters these buildings and visits the naves of which he may never have seen the like. It is perhaps, for this precise reason, that it is especially attractive and striking.

The oldest is Santa María la Blanca, which was constructed by the Arabs in the twelfth century. It has five narrow naves, separated from one another by rows of horse-shoe arches. The columns which support these arches are topped with plaster capitals, decorated with multi-colored plant motifs, which are never repeated throughout the entire synagogue. The Synagogue is crowned with a beautiful coffered larch ceiling.

As if they were made of stone, the capitals of Santa María la Blanca are carved from dry plaster. And even their origin has given rise to controversy. Some historians, as Gómez Moreno, claim that they are genuine though rather uncommon in the Arabic world, while other respected authorities, such as the Marqués de Lozoya, see in them, a Nordic derivation rooted in the Romanesque style.

Even though the temple was consecrated to Christianity at the beginning of the 15th century —somewhere around the years 1405—, its construction is believed to have been paid for by the tax collector of King Alfonso VIII, Rabbi Joseph, in the twelfth century.

It was certainly built by the Arabs —the second period of the Moslem architecture, which is appreciated in its Arabic transition style— for they left their mark within the attractive structure enclosed by the 32 pillars and the 28 horseshoe arches.

From then on, in other periods, Santa María la Blanca was a refuge for wayward ladies who had repented —Cardinal Siliceo designated it for that purpose in the 15th century— in order to become a military barracks at the end of the 18th century, and then a military storehouse. It was finally restored at the end of the 19th century.

Sephardic Museum. Cabalistic amulet.

Strictly Mudejar in style is the second synagogue, the Tránsito, and its construction, directed by Meir Abeli, was completed in 1366. Of very special interest is the Eastern wall with a superb lacework pattern, carved out of the stucco, and the tribunal extended along the right wall, which was where the women of the congregation were seated.

One of the Hebraic inscriptions which refer to the construction of the synagogue and which are carved out on the walls of the temple, speak of King Pedro I as "The Defender of the people of Israel". A frieze with coats of arms and new inscriptions quoting the Book of Psalms crown the side walls with 54 arches supported by columns and capitals of very unusual design.

After the expulsion of the Jews during the reign of the Catholic Monarchs, the temple was turned over to the Order of Calatrava in 1494 and it was then used as the Archives for this Order and the Order of Alcántara as well. It then became the Church of the Tránsito of Nuestra Señora. Today, it contains a Sephardic Museum and is considered a National Monument whose walls are covered with an enormous silk tapestry which was donated by an old Sephardic family.

THE TRANSITO SYNAGOGUE

In the 14th century, Samuel Levi, Treasurer of Pedro I the Cruel, constructed the Synagogue of the Tránsito. In it, we see the same decorative Mudejar elements as in Santa María la Blanca. It has a marvelous polychrome larch coffered ceiling and, on the walls, especially the front wall intended to guard the Torah, the Ataurique motifs and the Hebraic inscriptions are intermingled in an ornamental design of great beauty and elegance.

THE SEFARDI MUSEUM

The 13th of june of 1971, was inaugurated the Sefardi Museum of Toledo, inside The Tránsito Synagogue. Impregnated like any other one in Spain, whith Hebraic beings, the Sefardi Museum performes a reality that Spain can not forget. The collections of Sefardi Museum form two groups: A very important suits of epigraphs, most of them sepulchrals, proceeding from Toledo, León, Palencia, Madrid, Sevilla, etc. And another one of artistic, liturgical, folkloric and bibliographic objects given by private people and collections.

partial view. Santa María la Blanca Synagogue.

Plaster work of the Tránsito Synagogue.

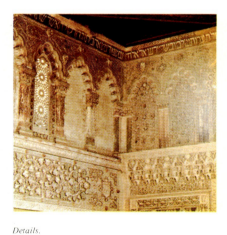

Details.

Sephardic museum.

A corner of the synagogue.

44

Cloister of San Juan de los Reyes.

Juan Guas was responsible for its construction and upon his death, Covarrubias continued the work. The end result was the sober and elegant building, considered as a masterpiece of Isabelline style, a building in which Gothic elegance blends with the Mudejar decoration. Perhaps we can appreciate this fusion of styles best in the two-story cloister: the lower level of flamboyant Gothic and the upper level, with Mudejar coffering. The beauty of this cloister will more than justify the visit to the Monastery.

San Juan de los Reyes owes its construction to a vow made by the Catholic Monarchs as they prayed for the Lord to grant them victory in the battle of Toro. The battle was won and the dispute over the throne of Castile between Isabel la Católica and Juana la Beltraneja, who was supported by Alfonso V of Portugal, was finally settled.

As we regard the main facade, our attention is immediately drawn to the rows of chains hanging from the wall, which represent the end of the Moslem domination of our land. These were the shackles of the Christians held pri-

Vaulted ceilings and choir of San Juan de los Reyes.

SAN JUAN DE LOS REYES

The traveller who comes to Toledo seeking art and history cannot afford to miss the Monastery of San Juan de los Reyes, which was founded by the Catholic Monarchs, Ferdinand and Isabella, as the place for their burial.

Palace of La Cava. In the background, San Juan de los Reyes.

The arcade of the cloister's upper gallery San Juan de los Reyes.

Doorway of the San Juan de los Reyes church.

Upper gallery of the San Juan de los Reyes cloister.

Facade of the San Juan de los Reyes church.
The chains of the Christian prisoners.

than Cardinal Jiménez de Cisneros, a historical fact which reflects the significance of the Monastery of San Juan de los Reyes to the city of Toledo and to all of Spain a well.

Here, also, we see a variety of styles despite the fact that it was "a complete church, made all in one go": Mudejar, Plateresque, Isabelline... It is, thus, a just representation of the broad artistic communication that only the Imperial City is capable of offering us.

San Juan de los Reyes, thanks to its fine restoration, maintains today all of its grace and magnificence. And we can still see the chains hanging from the wall which are today "more highly prized because of their historical value, than if they were made of gold!"

Cloister of San Juan de los Reyes.

soner in Ronda until the Catholic Monarchs were able to free that city from Moorish occupation. Many of the chains brought back to Toledo have long since disappeared, either stolen or destroyed, as in 1808, when the Napoleonic forces set fire to many buildings in Toledo, including this magnificent monastery, before they abandoned the city.

In addition, many works of art have also disappeared, such as the main altarpiece and other retables belonging to the side chapels, as well as a series of valuable paintings. The main altarpiece was replaced by another one taken from the Santa Cruz Hospital, and on either side of the transsept are the royal tribunes with the initials of Isabella and Ferdinand and their coats of arms carved in stone.

The Franciscan Order which took charge of the Monastery after its foundation has remained there over the centuries. Its first novice was none other

View of San Juan de los Reyes. ➔

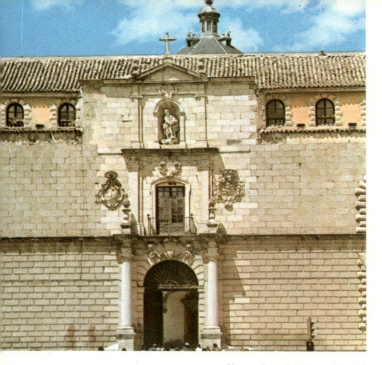

Upper gallery of the Tavera Hospital.

THE TAVERA HOSPITAL

The visitor can take a walk outside of the walled-in area and visit the Hospital de Tavera, where he can see a beautiful patio of late Spanish Renaissance style and admire two masterpieces by Berruguete, the entrance to the church, made entirely in Carrara marble and the sepulcher of Cardinal Tavera, founder of the hospital. There is also a magnificent picture gallery with works by Ribera, Zurbarán, Tiziano and many others, among whom "El Greco" can certainly not be lacking.

Also called the Hospital de Afuera (Hospital of the Outskirts) because of its location —we should remember the "Plano de Toledo" (Map of Toledo), traced by El Greco— its architects were

a relative of the founder, Nicolás Bustamante, who was a Jesuit priest, Hernán González de Lara and the Vergara family: the Elder and the Boy. Upon the death of Cardinal Tavera, the construction was delayed a great deal. The building passed over to the hands of the Lerma House in the 17th century but its main facade was not finished until the 18th century.

The temple, like the entire building, is dedicated to St. John the Baptist. Alonso de Berruguete took two years to complete the Cardinal's tomb, from 1559 to 1561. This was the year of the artist's death and he died in the little room at the main entrance, directly under the clock.

A museum nowadays, the left wing of the building was used as the stately dwelling of the Duke of Lerma. We will mention among the works by José Ribera, his suprising painting "La mujer barbuda" (The bearded lady), a portrait of a Neopolitan woman, Magdalena Ventura. The lady in question is shown sporting a long, full beard, and she is breast-feeding one of her children, while her husband regards her with a look of resignation. The other exceptional painting we cannot overlook is the "Sagrada Familia" (Holy Family), by Tintoretto which is found in the bedroom of the Duchess. We cannot forget the valuable 16th century chemist's shop as well as the Dining Room of Honor.

When we return to the center of town, we should head for the Puerta del Sol of which we have two views on the next page. Its name can possibly be attributed to the fact that it is oriented towards the West or to the drawing of the Sun and the Moon painted on the red marble which appears on the second arch, above a triangular coat of arms showing the Virgin presenting St. Ildephonse with the Chasuble. Its two battlemented keeps, one round and one square, represent together with the Bisagra Gate, the most beautiful entrances into the city.

The bearded woman by Ribera

← *The Baptising of Christi by Greco.*

Patio of the Alcázar.

Statue of the Emperor Carlos V.

ALCAZAR

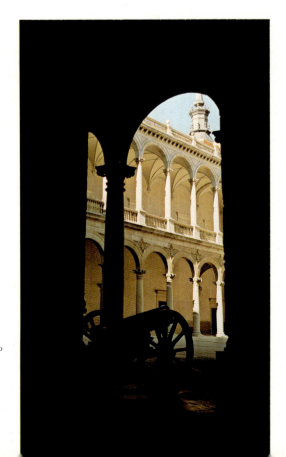

A view of the patio of the Alcázar.

The Alcázar.

Its reconstruction has been carried out in accordance with the original designs drawn up by Covarrubias. In the central patio, the visitor can admire the magnificent equestrian statue of Carlos V and in the esplanade, before the main entrance, the modern sculpture of Juan de Avalos.

It is situated on the highest and most strategic position of the city and so it served as a citadel for the Romans, Visigoths and Arabs. Alonso de Covarrubias, Francisco Villalpando, Juan de Herrera, and other important architects, participated in the later work and in 1882 it became a Military Academy.

Set on fire in 1710 by the English and Portuguese troops who supported the Archduke of Austria, it became a Charity House in 1772 under Cardinal Lorenzana, and was set on fire once again by the Napoleonic forces in the following century.

A stone's throw away from the Alcázar is the Hospital de Santa Cruz which is today an outstanding museum.

THE ALCAZAR

Our walk should come to a halt before the imposing presence of the Alcázar of Toledo. Someone wrote the following lines as he regarded the structure:

"If Toledo is a symbol of Spain, the Alcázar is the symbol of Toledo. If Toledo seems like a city cradled in the enormous hands of the surrounding hills which offer the city up to the Castilian sky as if it were the communion wafer, the Alcázar is like the soul of Toledo, like the magnificent Monstrance which is carried about on the shoulders of the faithful on Corpus Christi Day.

The building dates back to the beginning of our history (the third century) and ever since its foundation, it has been set aside for military uses. Perhaps for this reason, it has suffered the passage of time and the violence of Man like no other monument. The last time was during the Civil War when the Alcázar was almost entirely destroyed.

A view of the Alcázar.

The Alcázar. Southern facade.

CRISTO DE LA LUZ

Right beside the Puerta del Sol is one of the oldest buildings in Toledo for it was built during the very beginning of the Arab presence in Spain. For this reason, it lacks any flamboyant decoration which is characteristic of the later periods of Moorish art.

Its picturesque facade contains three doorways; the central one, with a half-point arch, the one on the left with a lobulated arch and the one on the right with a horse-shoe arch. Above the doorway is a body of blind horse-shoe arches and finally a simple lattice window.

The entire structure is made up of brick and stucco on the inside and it also has a colorful legend surrounding it.

In this case, it has not one but really two legends. It is said that the Christians, fearful of an attack by the Arab troops under Tarik, hid the Crucifixion, which was worshipped at a church near the Valmardón gate, in a hollow opening in one of the walls and put a small oil lamp at its feet. All of this took place at the beginning of the eighth century, while at the end of the eleventh, Alfonso VI and El Cid reconquered the city.

The Holy Familly, by Greco. "Tavera Hospital".

Cristo de la Luz mosque.

As they made their triumphant entrance into Toledo, the horses of both heroes came to a halt before the mosque and fell to their feet. The Bishop of Toledo, Don Bernardo, asked for permission to investigate the reasons behind such an unusual occurrence. When the building was opened and searched, the Crucifix was discovered... And the lamp at its feet was still burning after more than three hundred years!

Another legend, prior in time to the one we have just related, shows that during the reign of Atanagildo, two Jews, Sacao and Abisain, struck the Christ with a lance. The image began to bleed and the horrified men buried it in a barn. However, the blood stains led to the discovery of the crime, and the men were punished. For revenge, some other Jews smeared the foot of the Christ with lethal posion so that anyone who touched it would die. But the Crucifix, in order to avoid the tragedy, unnailed its foot from the cross and that is how we see it today.

This mosque has two sections with nine cupolas and six little naves interlaced in the first section, and twelve arches which support the ceiling.

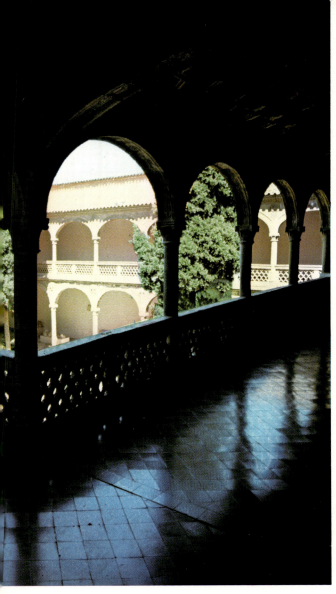

Upper gallery of the Santa Cruz Hospital.

THE
SANTA CRUZ HOSPITAL

In 1504, the first stone was put in place by Enrique Egas, the building's first architect, and the construction lasted for some ten years. Cardinal Mendoza, its promoter, did not live to see the symbolic act but the illustrious executor of his will, the Catholic Queen. Isabella,

put all her enthusiasm into carrying out the pet project of her advisor and confessor.

Its main Plateresque facade represents a prodigious sample of Spanish art and if, at first, it was a charity center for foundling children and for the ill, it has become to date a museum with nine very interesting rooms.

In the first room, we can admire the panels of Juan de Correa. In the second, the copy of Titian's portrait of Carlos V, painted by Juan Pantoja de la Cruz and many valuable documents.

The flags and banners of the Battle of Lepanto flagship preside over the third room which contains a portrait of Don Juan de Austria and an enlargement of the battle plan which is kept in the Simancas archives; and a bust of the Emperor in gilded silver which stands in the center of the room. In the fourth, we see a "Calvary", by Antonio Moro and the "Christ tied to the column", by Luis de Morales.

On the upper floor, in the fifth room, is a retable carved in wood by Alonso de Berruguete and a Crucifixion by Luis Tristán, monstrances, chalices and 17th century Belgian tapestries, with mythological scenes. In room six, attention should be especially directed to the "Holy Family in Nazareth" and the "Descent of Christ", by Jose de Ribera.

Room number seven is without a doubt the most important in the museum and it is known as the El Greco room because of the important collection of valuable material: original works, replicas and copies of the "Toledo's Greek", including the treasured "La Asunción", a major work belonging to his final period, opposite which is a showcase displaying the death certificate of the famous painter.

In Room number eight, we can see several privileges granted by Alfonso X and Alfonso VII, and some tapestries featuring the History of Alexander Magnum. The last room contains the "Cristo en la Cruz", attributed to Goya.

General view of the city. ⇒

*Site of the bath of La Cava and San Juan de los Reyes
in the background.*

OTHER MONUMENTS

But Toledo is endless when it comes to monuments. Next on the list are the City Council building, the old University, the San Servando castle, the Basilica of Santa Leocadia and the Cristo de la Vega, with its charming legend of Christ with the un-nailed right hand which inspired famous writer Zorilla; the Castle of Galiana, whose gardens were frequented by the Princess of the same name, daughter of Galafre, the Arab King or Governor of Toledo; the Archbishop's Palace in the Cathedral square; Santiago del Arrabal, behind the Bisagra gate; the old Dominican convent of San Pedro Mártir; Mozarabic Church of San Lucas, San Andrés and Santo Domingo el Antiguo monastery, place of "El Greco" burial and his genuine sanctuary. Santo Domingo el Antiguo was the lattest public museum opened. This museum has three pictures of "El Greco".

We can stop at the Baño de la Cava (Bath of La Cava), a keep which sinks its foundations into the river, a little beyond the San Martín bridge. This tower was once part of the support for the old San Martín bridge which was carried away by the flood waters in 1203.

It is said that the daughter of Count Julián, Florinda La Cava, chose this spot to bathe in the river, thinking that no-one could see her. One day, the last Visigothic monarch, Don Rodrigo, saw her and was so taken by her beauty that he fell upon her and made her his lover. Angered by the attack on his daughter, the legend —which is in this case entirely false— explains, Don Julián, Mayor of the Fort of Ceuta, joined forces with the Arabs in order to defeat Rodrigo in the battle of Guadalete.

Puerta del Sol. →

Puerta del Cambrón. →

ain façade of the Santa Cruz Hospital.

City walls.

The Santa Ursula "cigarral" (country home).

THE "CIGARRALES", COUNTRY HOUSES

Another significant aspect of Toledo is found in the surrounding countryside: The "Cigarrales". These marvelous homes, set in the midst of hectares of farmland, offer the ideal setting for rest, relaxation and meditation.

Among the olive trees, the furrows, the shadows, the water well and the fruit trees surrounding the house. The Toledans or friends of Toledo lead their lives with a special mysticism.

"... in addition to this, as there are valleys, hills, many *cigarrales* and country homes..." This is perhaps the first time that the word "cigarral" is printed and it appears in the "Memorial Report on the outstanding characteristics of the Imperial City of Toledo", by Luis Hurtado de Mendoza. This was in the year 1576.

The *cigarrales* are the properties located on the outskirts of the city which may furnish the owner with a place for rest and relaxation, but meager or non-existent financial profits.

For some, the origin of the word is Arabic, even though the Dictionary of the Royal Academy of the Spanish Language says it comes from the word "cigarra" (cricket), for there is an abundance of these insects in summer and their shrill noise fills the air. Still others claim that the origin of the word comes from the fact that part of the clergy came to these slopes on the outskirts of town to smoke cigarettes, an activity which the Archbishop had prohibited. Or perhaps it comes from the word "ciegarreales" (Blinded), which is a clear reference to its limited profitability.

Sebastián de Covarrubias, in his "Treasure of the Castilian Language", defines the "cigarrales" as "properties located on the hills not far from the center of town and which were ordinarily small plots of land. The most important *cigarrales* have fountains, dry fruit trees, a small vineyard, olive groves, fig trees and a little house". They are located on the left bank of the Tagus.

A view of the inside.

rrabal quarter and Bisagra Gate.

The National Parador of "Conde de Orgaz".

GASTRONOMY.
RECOMMENDATIONS

Toledo, throughout the province, treasures a series of delicious specialties which are openly enticing; some dishes are unique to the area, while others are shared with different regions of our geography.

Of course, if it were necessary to single out just one of the original dishes of the region, we would all choose the stuffed partridge Toledo style, a perennial specialty of the famous "Venta de Aires". If this is the place you have chosen for your meal, you can begin with another typical dish which is certainly worthwhile: "the potato omelette *a la magra*", a juicy omelette "mounted" on a tasty piece of loin pork.

Another characteristic dish, the quail with lima beans, is among the specialties of the "Hostal del Cardenal", a splendid, 18th century palace which has been suitably decorated and which stands beside the Bisagra gate. This restaurant is under the same management as Madrid's traditional Botín restaurant, which guarantees that the lamb and pig will be roasted in an oven which is identical to the world famous oven of the Madrid restaurant. Partridge stew, when in season, is a treat in any of the city's restaurants and the magnificently marinated partridge can be enjoyed all year round.

We must also mention the "Conde de Orgaz" National Inn opened not too long ago. It is housed in a structure which fits in ideally with the setting, on the other side of the river, along the Paseo de los Cigarrales, and the Parador organizes its unforgettable medieval dinners periodically.

Also highly recommendable are "Chirón" and "Casa Aurelio", which offer a delicious garlic soup or vegetable stew along with all the other specialties we mentioned. We cannot overlook the garlic chicken or garlic rabbit and the asparagus omelette at the "El Emperador", set amidst the *cigarrales*. The exotic flavor of the Jewish food served with kosher wine is available at the Sinai restaurant in the heart of the Jewish quarter; the contrast between good cooking in a refined atmosphere facing El Greco's house, at "El Porche"; "Adolfo" set up in an old house with a medieval coffered ceiling; "El Patio" found in a Toledo palace; the romantic setting of "El Siglo 19"; and La Tarasca, settled next to the Cathedral.

For dessert, the "marquesita", the "rusos", the "melindres" and the marzipan, which was invented in Toledo when the city was under siege by Alfonso VI. It is said that the Arabs mixed sugar and ground almonds to prepare a treat to sweeten the lives of the defenders of the city. Special attention should also be given to the Manchego goat chese coming from all over the province and the neighboring villages of La Mancha. And the savory wines from, for example, Noblejas, Méntrida or Dos Barrios.

Outdoor display of handicraft work.

TOLEDO HANDICRAFTS

Toledo's attractions are limitless and it is and has always been a city and a province of artistic and artisan skill par excellence. The Damascene work, for example, the *ataujía*, was created in Egypt perhaps but it had schools in Greece, Rome and Byzantium, for the art of inlaying fine metals on iron and steel. This practice was brought to Spain by the Arabs and its name in Spanish, *damasquinado*, appears to be a derivation of the name of Damascus. The work reached extraordinary levels of refined mastery in Toledo. Today, together with monstrances, chalices, chests and swords, we find all kinds of utensils with Damascene work, such as cufflinks, tie clasps, pins, cases...

We cannot mention swords without going into the whole history behind the sword in Toledo. In his work "Viaje a España" (Trip to Spain), between 1786 and 1787, Joseph Townsend wrote of his visit to the Royal Arms Factory: "The steel there is of excellent quality and so perfectly tempered that if the blade were held tightly against a shield, it would bend like a whale, and yet it is capable of cutting through a helmet without damaging the blade".

Brotherhoods and guilds have existed over the years in Toledo until the present day, when hundreds of shops and bazaars fill the streets and squares with a fine array of artistic wares.

The long history of the city can be found in the variety of crafts offered: woven work, embroidery, engravings, wrought iron work, carvings and, in a very special manner, the clay and ceramic work, not to mention the other handicrafts we have already mentioned. The rosary of names, such as Talavera de la Reina, Lagartera, Puente del Arzobispo, Escalona, Oropesa, open with generosity, splendor and promise to the four corners of the province.

So Toledo is an eminently artistic land, with an incomparable variety of treasures, which the native craftsmen handle with the same loving care and devotion as their ancestors did centuries ago.

Display of local craft work.

Toledo: Rocky Gravity. ⇉

Maqueda castle (Province of Toledo). ⇉